REBOUND

*How to Bounce Back and
Disrupt your Market with
Strategic Innovation*

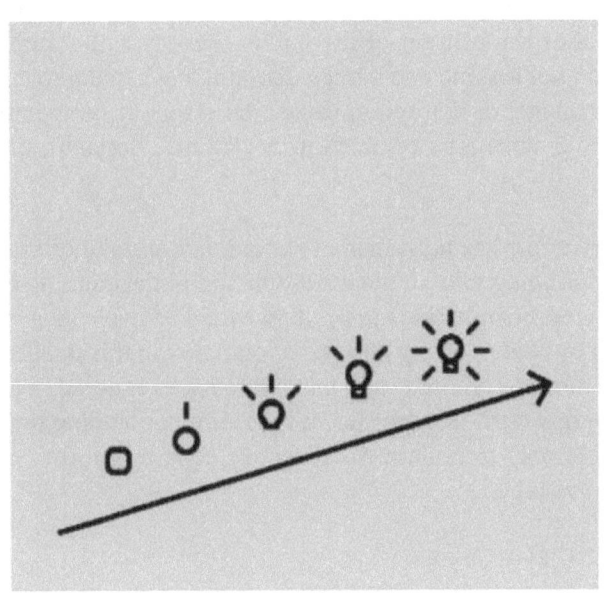

UTSSAV GUPTA

notionpress
.com

INDIA · SINGAPORE · MALAYSIA

Notion Press

No.8, 3rd Cross Street
CIT Colony, Mylapore
Chennai, Tamil Nadu – 600004

First Published by Notion Press 2020
Copyright © Utssav Gupta 2020
All Rights Reserved.

ISBN 978-1-64828-774-9

For information please contact the author at:

rebound@utssavgupta.com

DISCLAIMER

The author and the publisher of this book have researched all information contained in this book for motivational self-help and educational purposes to buyers across the globe. In an event of any inconsistency or inaccuracy with respect to any information in this book, the author and the publisher will not be liable for such error that might have occurred in the book either by way of negligence of any kind or by any other causes as the case may be, causing damage to the reader either or indirectly.

The content of this book is solely based on the author's opinions, ideas, experiences, and views; which does not in any way come from the point of view of an expert or professional in the field; therefore, the opinion of the author should not be substituted by the reader for any professional, legal, and psychological help and advice the reader could get from an expert. Thus, in a situation when the content of this book is adopted; and it causes damage, disruption will not be made to indemnify such buyer for adopting a method in this book causing damage.

The author shall not grant any warranty or guaranty either implied or expressed to the buyer as to the context of this book. As a result of which neither the author nor the publisher shall be liable for any damage meted on the reader by way of using the information provided within the chapter of this book. To this extent, the author is free entirely from bearing any liability of any sort arising from the usage of this book, since it is based on the personal testimony of the author.

All companies referred to in this book are basically for reference purposes and are not meant to be interpreted as malicious in anyway, by reason of which the Author and publisher of this book shall not be held liable in defamation of character for the mode of writing adopted by the Author.

Dedicated to

YOU

THANKS TO

My late father, Mr. Rajiv Gupta, who by example taught the power of principle.

My mother, Mrs. Mukta Gupta, for her unwavering faith, passion and strength by which my upbringing was shaped.

To my wife Parul, son Anay, family Mayank and Nishtha for their unconditional support, inspiration and sacrifice.

To my friends and peers who were with me throughout, encouraging, validating and keeping me grounded.

My heartfelt thanks to Master Kamlesh D. Patel (Daaji) and HH Goswami Shri Dwarkeshlalji Maharaj Shri for whom I had the great fortune of working for. They inspired me deeply, and it is with their blessing that I could complete this work.

To my coaches Akshar Yadav and Avy Loren Cohen for not only training me in the necessary skills, but for also being wonderful friends. This would not have been possible without their warm encouragement and push.

To my clients who instilled the drive of finding solutions. Their sharing, their asks that often lead me to think out of box and their faith in me has helped build up the acumen.

There are always a special few, ones who come into our lives as elders, teachers and mentors, who subtly instil suggestions and inspirations. These silent voices slip deep into the subconscious and have shaped my inner paradigm. My immense gratitude to those who I have been so fortunate to have during my journey.

Last but not the least, I thank the Almighty who has so graciously showered his blessings and has given me strength to keep persevering even in hard times.

Table of Contents

Chapter 1

THE FUTURE OF YOUR BUSINESS DEPENDS ON THIS

Would you like to capture more market share?

Do you find that despite having a stable stream a few years ago, your business is not really growing?

As an entrepreneur, you have tried everything that came your way. You have a good sales team, your systems are updated, you have a training budget and constantly invest in yourself and your team; you have great networks, yet results don't show up.

What is it that stops your business from attaining a sizable market?

Why is it that even when there is a demand, your product is not able to get a bigger chunk of the market?

If questions like these keep you up at night, then you are in the right place. In this book, I am going to reveal the secret behind major success stories and tell you what the businesses are doing that have disrupted the market.

> *Let's look at Google. Ever wondered why it continues to evolve ever since it was founded? For those who remember the wee days, companies like Yahoo, AltaVista and MSN used to dominate the search engine market. Google came up with a better and more efficient method to catalogue internet sites and yield faster search results. It constantly*

kept upgrading and expanding its services even though it was a fairly new player. And now, even when it is at its peak and an undisputed giant of the internet world, it does not stop innovating for new and better products.

This is the secret of Google's success.

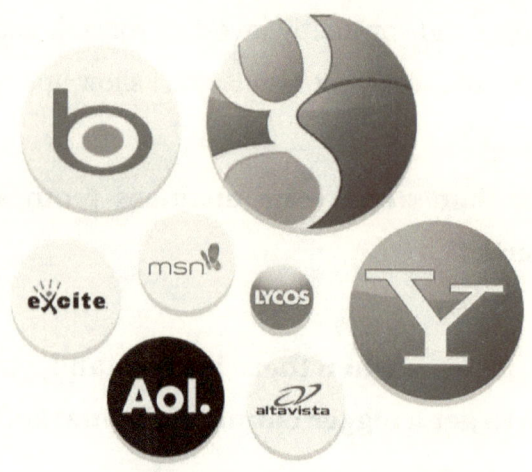

Google with its major competititors

Innovation has taken an unprecedented role in today's modern era. In the drastically changing world of technological advancement, innovation has created conditions for the emergence of new niches. The more these niches it has created, more opportunities get generated to further innovate.

While innovation continues to be the bedrock of new businesses, they seem to find it hard to achieve.

In a survey conducted by Mckinsey & Company, 86% of global business executives believe innovation is extremely important and yet, only 6% of them are satisfied with their innovation performance.

What is worrisome is that innovation remains a black box mystery to most and is not really understood in any depth.

Forbes published an article '**90% Of Indian Startups Will Fail Because Of Lack Of Innovation, Study Says,**' where they conducted a survey and found that despite having the third largest ecosystem for startups, 77% of venture capitalists believe that they lack unique business models and new technology.

In this book, I will talk about:

- What makes even established businesses, products, and services lose their market share.
- Why constant innovation is so important for business's growth.
- What challenges entrepreneurs face while making decisions that lead companies to incorrect directions.
- How innovation can be applied as a problem-solving tool to achieve a deep level impact on the market.

Brace yourselves as we dive in, and keep taking notes in your journal of revelations you have during the read.

From Subjectivity to Objectivity

My quest for innovation began during my high school days, gaining piece by piece as I went through stages of education, profession and life.

I was trained at the best architectural schools at Delhi and London and was exposed to the design world from an early age, coming from a family of architects. It was due to this that I found myself in a state of deep query towards the subjectivities and contradictions that the design field possesses in cultural landscapes.

> *What defines right fit and how do you find it?*
>
> *Why is it that an idea or a decision that seems perfectly relevant today turns out otherwise tomorrow?*
>
> *What are the right metrics for decision making?*
>
> *How to derive objective truth from subjectivities?*

These questions led me to study disciplines like business design, innovation and strategies in search of the missing pieces. The more I looked, the deeper it took me into the rabbit hole.

I found myself not alone in the search for answers. As it happens, many innovation researchers have also been asking similar questions, and they have some pretty good answers.

Life presents inspirations in mysterious ways.

My company got caught in the changing market dynamics and plunged to an all-time low. It was then I realised the true potential of innovation and what it can do. We chose to restructure our business using innovation concepts. As a result, the company got revived; it is growing and now doing projects of the kind we had never thought of before.

The proof of the concept came from our own case.

Since then, I have spent years studying and honing innovation frameworks that we used for clients to help them look at their business cases differently. It has profoundly changed how we design architecture and has put us in the forefront of cutting-edge infrastructure.

In this book, I share the knowledge acquired by studying companies from around the globe and their strategies.

The Eureka Moment(s)

Thomas Edison tried and failed nearly two thousand times before developing carbonized cotton thread filament for the incandescent light bulb. When asked about it, he said, "I did not fail, I found 2000 ways how not to make a light bulb. I only needed to find one to make it work."

Edison's perseverance after each failure - with positivity and purpose - turned failures into learning opportunities, to gain more insights and flip the curve back up towards success.

Look at the graph below. This is how typically businesses and products undergo the journey of ups and downs plotted across a time span. My spiritual side would like to call it the rhythmic sine curve of life because, like they say, "What goes up also comes down."

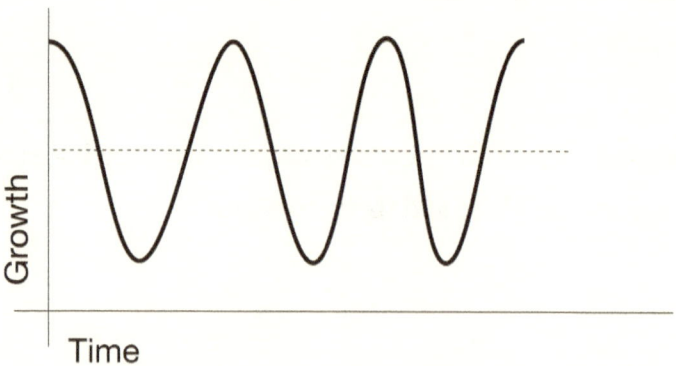

The figure below represents data from financial sector plotting the last hundred years. Notice how it is full of ups and downs, some being smaller, other having peaks and valleys on a larger scale.

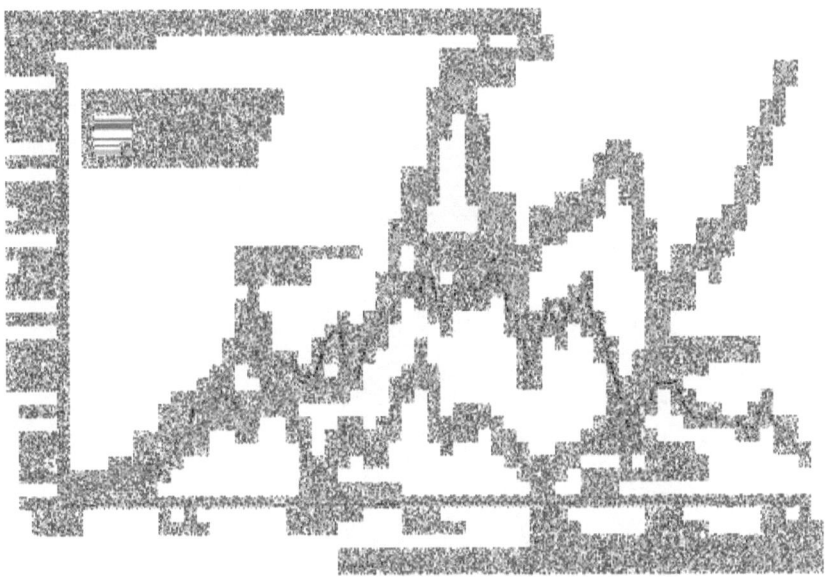

100 years of market cycle adjusted for inflation

(source:https://www.forbes.com/sites/greatspeculations/2015/01/15/ understand-markets-in-2015-with-these-15-charts/#5a73141665dc)

Here is the catch: rhythmic sign curves works differently for each entity depending on the companies' strategies and efforts. Some progressions lead to a gradual slowdown, others have excessive high and low moments that only increase in magnitude.

Segments like CFL and cars like the Ambassador went away, like the first curve below. Stock market behaviour is a perfect example of the second type.

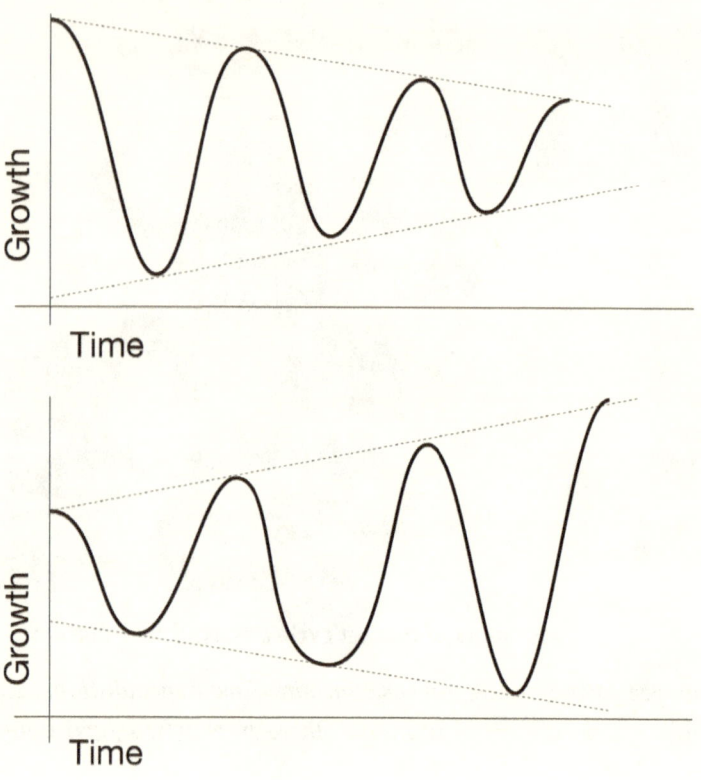

 Can you spot highs and lows in your business and map them chronologically? What kind of sign curve does it look like?

The question is, how can you change this curve in your favour and warp it for steady growth with least intensity lows and more highs?

Well, the answer is to convert low valleys into **'THRUST POINTS'**.

Puzzled? Let me explain this.

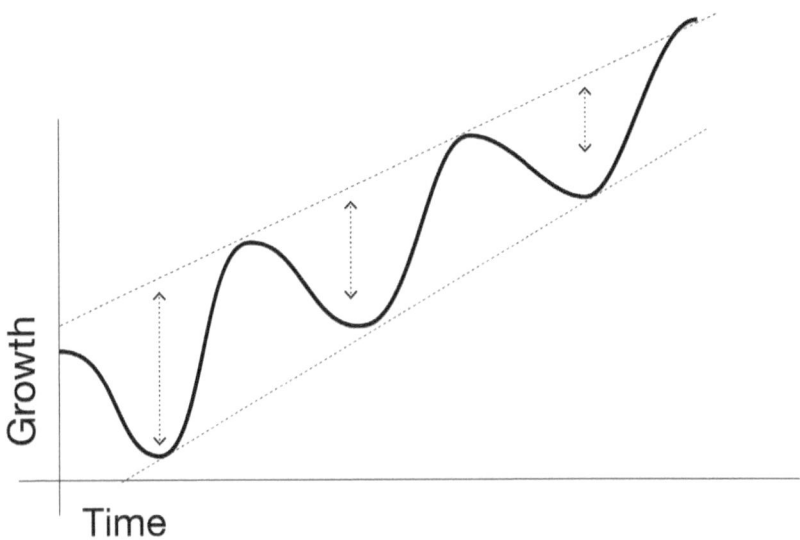

Morphed sign curve

Take a look at the graph above and compare it with previous diagrams. Notice something different? I'll give you a clue - observe the reduced length of time between the highest point to the lowest valley point.

Real opportunity presents during declining curves, revealing a mismatch, shortcoming or something that is not working right. Innovative companies look at these moments as diagnosis and endeavour to learn as much as they can. Like how a doctor who conducts a diagnosis using symptoms shown by our body.

Thomas Edison took every failure as learning and drew insights from them that led to his next steps. For products and services, a declining curve often indicates a certain forecast or a pattern representing change in consumer behaviour.

The whole idea is about tapping into this moment with the right speed and right intervention; this is the key to successful companies.

Such companies understand the importance of failure and how important they are for lessons in the long term. They develop a culture to embrace this moment and tap into its potential.

> *"Blame is not for failure, it is for failing to help or ask for help." The CEO of the Lego group, Jorgen Vig Knudstorp, explains about the company's culture.*

> *Google has a culture where people have no problem admitting that something is not working. Instead, they are encouraged to learn from it and pick up the pieces to further innovate.*

Observe in the graph again how, with each iteration, reaction time is decreased, resulting in a lower decline period and more upward soar. This is the result of a sharper approach and consistent effort.

It is about mindfully observing and making the right choices. Downward moments are nothing more than a blip, just a temporary phase that companies take as learning opportunities.

Chapter 2

THE BIG TRAP

In order to grow and sustain, companies aspire for the following.

- Expanding their market share

  Increase customer base

- Getting a better bracket of clients/customers

  Improving on revenue share per customer

- Capturing new markets

  Venture in allied markets

- Growth acceleration

  Increasing the rate of growth in market share

- Increasing profitability and ROI

  Improving costs, shortening the sales cycle and more sales cycle done at the same time

- Tackling declining segments

  Turning around non-profitable ventures

- Being future-ready

  Predicting trends.

When we look closely, companies are always dealing with evolving customer needs and competition. Irrespective of a company being an established one, like Boeing, or a new venture like start-up, itis not exclusive or limited to any sector or segment.

When sales don't go as planned, companies focus on three key problem objectives. Interestingly, below the surface, the real problem lies somewhere else.

Problem 1

Getting customers to buy your product/services.

Part of the problem is about understanding the right customer base for the product, but what really matters is making the product the right fit for customers' needs and jobs. This is where companies face product take-off issues.

Problem 2

Attaining a sizeable market share

Lack of distinguishing factors from those of your competitors creates the 'COMMODITY EFFECT' and thus make it harder to get customers/clients. When the value of your service/business is not clear and relevant, the products/services are a 'me too' option with no clear edge above other competing products.

Problem 3

Sustaining for the long-term

Competition and changing trends make the products or services unfit for users in due course. Even established companies struggle to keep up in the long term due to either of these factors.

Any business that has existed for over a decade has felt this phenomena at some point.

Let's take Microsoft as an example that illustrates the above. Having almost the entire market share in its early days of the 1990s, Microsoft began to lose its share to other evolving products. The server market shifted to Redhat, Unix and VMware. The MS-Office users shifted to online offices; even the desktop platform saw Mac and Linux as competition. This only worsened as more and more allocation got hosted on the web and did not depend on desktop operating systems to run.

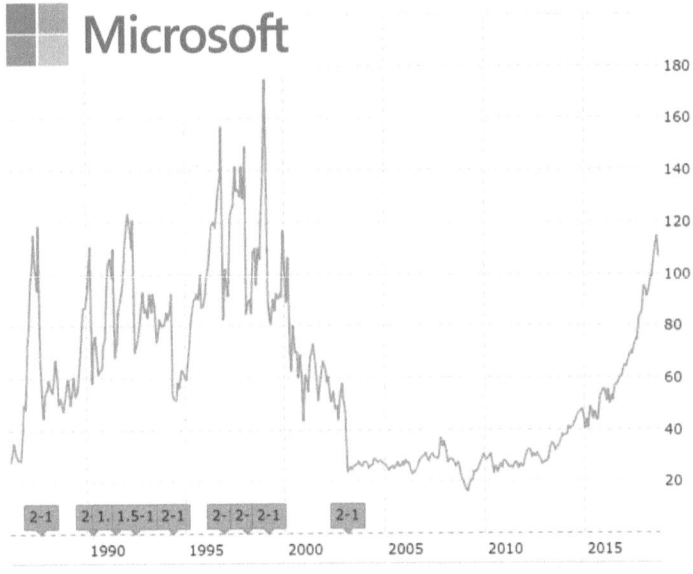

History of Microsoft Stock

(Source: https://www.benzinga.com/money/how-to-buy-microsoft-stock/)

Microsoft's stock graph in 1990 was at an all-time high and dropped in later years as a result of the above. It was only around 2012 that it started regaining as a result of something we are going to discuss later.

Traditional solutions ~~that works~~ that used to work

In order to meet sales targets and solve stagnation problems, companies use various strategies. At a high level, they are as follows.

- **Increase outreach**

    Creating more market awareness through campaigns, adverts, events, and social media. In case of business to business companies, they take more of a networking based approach. Improving sales processes like creating pitches, distributing sample kits and packets, etc, are other tactics companies use.

We all remember television commercials for detergents like Aerial and Nirma, and soaps like Lifebuoy.

NIRMA-washing powder nirma Advertisement Jingle

- **Play in pricing structure**

  Getting a better price through efficient supply chain system, penetrative pricing, offering deals or mass discounts to move the inventory and slashing prices to eliminate the competition have been a play most in the product industry do. This may diffuse the immediate problem, but this is not a long-term solution.

Chinese companies are experts in price wars. We will speak about pricing innovations later, but in this context, the price war has costed even the giants like Boeing and Sony millions of dollars.

- **Diversifying into other market segments**

  When one segment is not working properly due to internal or external conditions, companies tend to diversify into other segments.

Nike, the shoe brand, tried their hand in wearable technology with 'Fuel Band', a wearable bracelet that could track fitness activities. In this case, the primary segment of the company is stable, and this offshoot did not work. The product is still struggling, and Nike is finding ways to improve it.

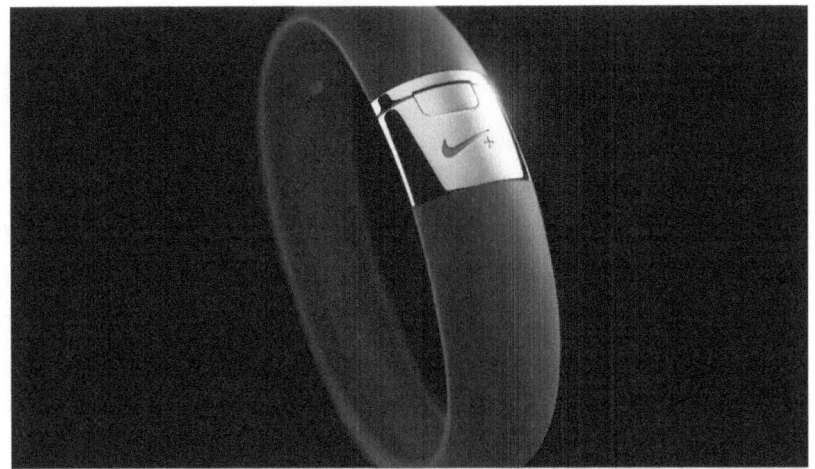

Most businesses tend to go for the first two strategies - to increase market awareness and to use pricing structure to get a push for their products/services. This may create an initial boost, but when outcomes do not stick fora longer period, it indicates another problem.

Some businesses go for diversification, to tap into other segments, but they too end up with the same core issues.

Though each one of the above strategies are good actionable plans having their own proven records, they all are meant for a specific purpose and therefore would not yield long-term results if applied in an incorrect context.

What really matters for the continual sustenance and growth of business is appropriateness of products or services. If the base product does not meet customer needs and experiences, other strategies do not help beyond a certain point.

> *Nokia was a pioneer in phone manufacturing for more than a decade. It was a very popular phone brand with as much as 80% of market share in some countries. By the mid-2000s, Nokia was without a match and it became the dominant player in all segments of devices. In 2008, a new generation of touch screen smartphones with business capability came into the market. Consumer requirements kept evolving for more sophisticated internet communicators. Products like iPhone and android OS development filled the void and essentially impacted*

> *Nokia's share. The demand for Nokia phones suddenly dropped. Despite their aggressive marketing, strategic moves like tying up with Microsoft for OS, and a few new releases, they could not regain the market despite their competitive pricing structure*

We will discuss more about the story of Nokia and their brilliant comeback in later chapters.

In 90% cases, businesses jump towards other methods without taking a relook at their offerings for their effectiveness and market desirability. Thus, they continue to struggle in the market, slow down, get rejected and even collapse.

The missing FOURTH DIMENSION that companies almost always seem to miss as a primary option is to re-engineer their products and services and to STRATEGICALLY INNOVATE.

 *Before moving forward, I would like you to take a moment and reflect upon the typical problems you face in business and the solutions adopted to resolve them.*

Even when innovation is the only solution, why are entrepreneurs still stuck?

The story of Kodak has many lessons to learn from. Kodak was once the biggest producer of camera films and dominated that market. Believe it or not, it was also the first company to invent the digital camera way back in 1975. Today, one can imagine what a huge opportunity they were sitting on.

Contrary to adopting this technology, management saw the invention as a threat to their existing line of business. They decided to kill it. It was not long before their competitors like Sony, Nikon, Olympus and Fuji Film developed digital camera technology of their own and capitalised on that. Kodak remained in denial and still kept betting on cameras with films. Kodak drastically lost their market share; by the time they decided to adopt digital cameras, it was already too late. The company filed for bankruptcy in 2012.

Looking back at the Kodak story, ever wondered why Kodak executives did not believe in the new technology? What made them feel so threatened about it that they turned a blind eye towards the digital camera segment for years?

Decline of Film

Film rolls sold

Camera sales

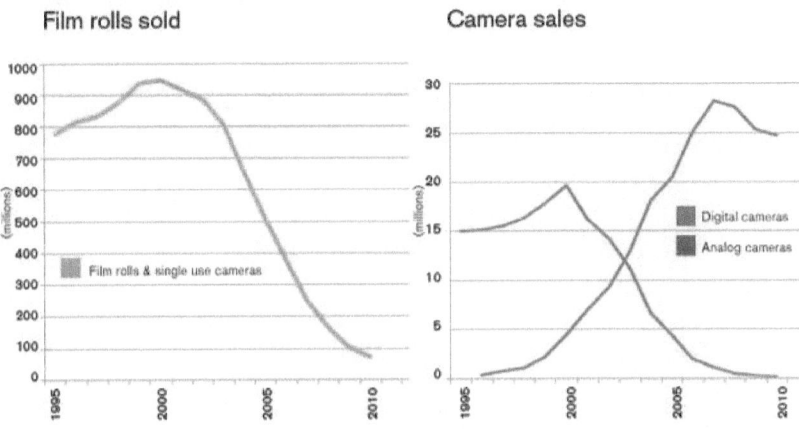

(Source: Jake Nielson via Twitter)

As it turns out, Kodak executives were focused on data from business spreadsheets that showed extremely promising sales of camera films. Any proposition of sacrificing these numbers for something that did not yet exist was something they could not be fathom. They simply could not see that far on the other side of the story.

Company executives and entrepreneurs face this moment of truth much too often: to weigh between what is surely in front of them and against betting on an unsure future that requires changes in current. This is the 'entrepreneurs' dilemma'.

> **Entrepreneurs' dilemma** *is a phenomenon when they are faced with these situations and must make decisions for the future of products or services without clear supporting factors.*

Now there are two cases here.

1: Immediate recognition

2: Slow burn.

The first case is for companies where the business structure, segment or the market are such that patterns are immediately recognisable. So the response towards the shift in strategy is more aggressive. For example, startups can adapt quickly towards the market events.

The second case is for more established companies and for long lead services/products - where preparation time or gestation periods are large. Results appear somewhat late and do not reflect the problem clearly in their early phases. In such cases, almost every time, executives are faced with making decisions in a grey area. Like in the case of Kodak and Kingfisher Airlines

In the words of nuclear physicist Edward Teller, *"Life improves slowly and goes wrong fast, and only catastrophe is clearly visible."*

This is the #1 reason for an entrepreneur's failure.

Had executives known about the future, would they have made the decision to kill digital camera research? Obviously not.

So how do you decide when to act and adopt the right strategy before it's too late?

How do business owners, enterprises and company executives seek cues for the future and make clear bets?

The answer lies in understanding what causes products to fail, ultimately leading to business failures.

 *Does your business show rapid indication or slow results? What are the dilemmas you face?*

Chapter 3

WHAT CAUSES PRODUCTS, SERVICES AND BUSINESSES TO FAIL

There are several reasons for why such a causality happens. But by far, the #1 reason lies in the relationship between the following three components.

- The Product
- The User or Market
- The Job.

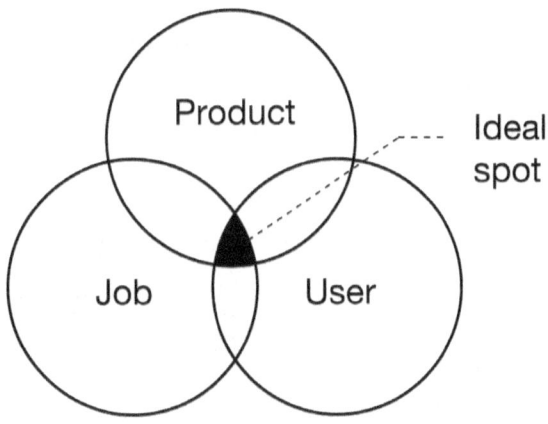

Let's take an example of 'business bags' to illustrate the above. Bags being the product created by companies like Samsonite, Carlton and alike; business users being the customer segment.

> *If we see what a business user would require - they need to carry one or two pairs of clothes, have slots to carry wires, laptops and notebook in something that is easy to wheel*

and gives an executive look. I am sure this is something every entrepreneur can relate to. This is what we call 'Job of the product', the physical activity or the solution users of that segment intend to get done by using that product.

Now imagine bags from twenty years back and using those to travel for business. Quite unimaginable, isn't it? Where do you safely stow your laptop? The bag is too big and cumbersome!

Now imagine one company comes up with a beautiful business bag, a small compact case with lots of space inside, which is easy to wheel. Would it not instantly attract customers?

This is what happens to products when they do not serve the job for the customers or their segments. The existing line of products deteriorate, but worse, someone from the competition would figure out and capture the market.

Bag industry companies created a **'business bag series'** using this fundamental to develop smaller bags that had waterproof fabric or leather with lots of pockets. These products further evolved as the job evolved. Like from shoulder straps preference to two-wheel drag and later to four-wheel push, and even slots for iPads and charger wires when the use of mobility devices increased.

Conventional bags

New business bags

Clearly, there is a relationship between the users, the job and the product.

> Let's continue with the bag industry example. Say Company A has a business bag series and another Company B who does not. If you were to buy a new bag for business travel, which one would you go for?

> Would your decision change if Company B is aggressively promoting their luggage pieces and have even offered huge discounts on it?

Obviously not.

You may take the benefit of the sale price to buy for holiday travel, but not for business.

Successful businesses lies in the intersection of the three.

Stagnation or disparity between any single component creates the divergence, which is the root cause of undesirability, eventually leading to product failure.

 *What is the job that the customer is trying to get done using your products or services?*

This brings us to the next point - why is it that products that were successful earlier could not sustain in today's time? As it turns out, *users' needs and jobs are constantly evolving* as a result of the following three components.

- Trends
- Direct competitors and their offerings
- Indirect competitors and their offerings.

There is a common belief that successful companies possess the right product in the right category at the right time. They somehow belong to a segment that is lucrative and does not face competition.

Let's take an example from the music industry that illustrates the above two points.

> *Music sharing started with records as the media, which created the record player market. When the tape was invented, cassettes took over the market, and the player market changed. As their popularity grew, portable players were introduced that were battery operated, which people could take along in their cars and on holidays. In early 1990, Sony introduced a portable personal cassette player device called the Walkman.*

In the 2000s, the media changed to CDs and thus made the market for cassette tapes obsolete. Take a look at how CDs took over the market from cassette tapes.

Until now, only a direct competitor was making these changes from within the same industry. But what was about to happen next was unprecedented. The digital player market was growing and pretty much the next leap players with internal memory. The MP3 player was an early contender, but when Apple's iPod came out, it not only brought in an incremental jump in the player's capacity and style, but changed the concept of buying music with iTunes. Now, users had an option to buy a single track rather than buying the entire album. They could even rent the track.

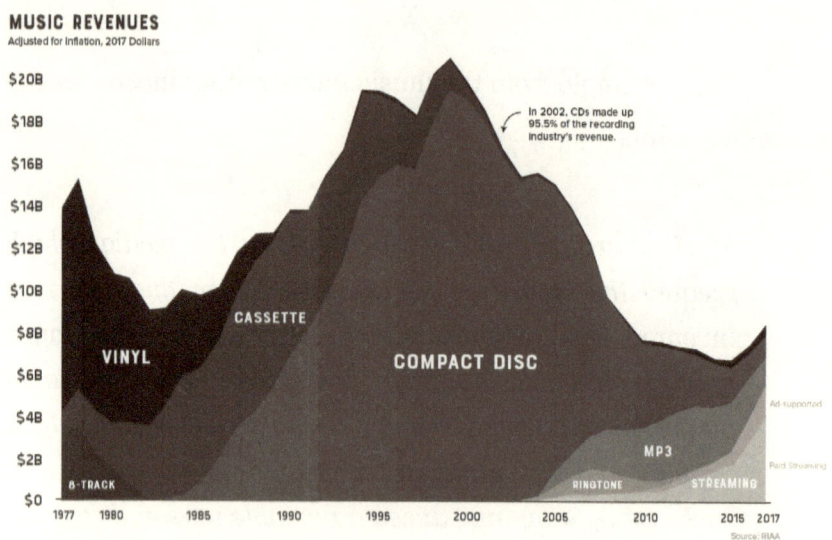

(*Source: www.visualcapitalist.com/music-industry-sales/*)

The graph below shows how revenue patterns changed with the above described model of buying.

So, an indirect competitor entered the market from a different segment and created a new niche that killed all their competitors and changed the market as a whole. The story does not stop here. Post 2008, as the mobile phone market revolutionised, music got integrated with mobile devices and had now got an advantage of internet streaming. So not only did the standalone player market get disrupted, but a whole new web-based provider niche was born. Companies like Spotify, Prime Music and Last FM changed the way people consumed music.

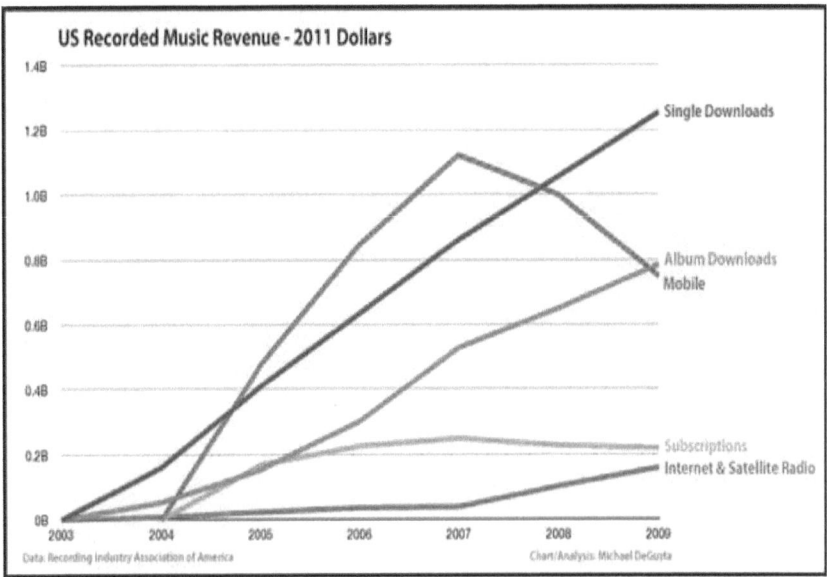

(Source: Nevoda's the business of new media)

Notice how, in this example, the segment of the market remained dominated with conventional music media and this suddenly changed as a result of indirect competition. Consumer electronics giants like Sony and Samsung and distribution channels like stores and music parlours got extinct thanks to this segment.

So what should companies do to cope with the changing consumer landscape?

Introducing 'The Blade'

Remember Y2K?

In the year 2000, when the world entered the new millennium, the Y2K threat was looming above the computer industry, making financial markets very worried. What followed was a boom in the dot com world; thereafter came the information revolution brought about by companies like Google and YouTube, and then social connectivity by companies like Facebook and Twitter.

This was not limited to just the IT segment. Apple had already disrupted the market by their new generation Mac, the revolutionary iPod and later, in 2008, by the iPhone. All three belonged to consumer electronics from three different categories. And while many companies perished in the 2008 economic crash, companies like Apple, Google and Facebook not only survived but continued to thrive.

If we try to find a pattern here, all these examples belong from different industries, all of them catered to a diverse range of user segments, all of them have a different problem they are trying to solve. So what is the common denominator? Why did they keep growing when other companies took a hit? Was it luck or a unique strategy?

It was **Strategic Innovation** that placed these companies in a zone of growth.

Constant innovation is required to cope with the rapidly changing landscape. Innovation presents a solution to look at the business problems differently. Its theories create models that, through a systematic approach, can lead to solve the root of the problem.

> *Let's see how an innovative mindset would rephrase the problems that we discussed above. Take a look at the table on the next page. Notice how, by changing the questions, new directions start to show up. We will discuss more about this in 'Power of Questioning'.*

	Typical problem statement	Redefined problem	Solution
1	How to **get customers to buy** your products/ services.	How to **get the right product** the customer would like to buy.	
	"GET CUSTOMERS TO BUY"	"GET THE RIGHT PRODUCT"	Creating products/ services that customers need.
2	**Attaining** a **sizable** market **share**.	**Attracting** more **customers** to build a sizable market share.	
	ATTAINING SIZEABLE SHARE	ATTRACTING more CUSTOMERS	Beat the commodity effect by creating a unique and relevant niche
3	**Sustaining long term**	**Constantly evolving** towards changing trends, needs and competitors.	
	SUSTAIN BUSINESSES	CONSTANTLY EVOLVE	Strategic innovation to constantly evolve products and offerings.

Crossroads or low points, which we discussed in Chapter 1, are important decision points where businesses can take a new course to reinvent themselves. Only 2% of companies see these crossroads as an opportunity to grow and choose using innovation to reengineer and develop their products/services.

Strategic Innovation not only helps in growth by relooking at the products/services, but also helps in sustaining by tackling impact from competition in the future. A mindset of innovation always looks for the right questions and looks for possibilities.

 Take a moment to phrase the problem statement and rephrase the questions in the above format.

For example, you have a business for real estate development and your current issue is to get customers to buy your development offering.

A standard question would look like this:

"How can I get the customers to buy my units?"

A redefined question would look like this:

"What can I build that the customers would like to buy?"

Don't limit yourself when redefining the question. If redefined questions make you uncomfortable and make you feel like you are stepping out of your comfort zone, then you are moving in the right direction. Stay with me; all the answers are there in the coming chapters.

Chapter 4

UNBOXING INNOVATION

"Innovation distinguishes between a leader and a follower."
(Steve Jobs, 2005)

When Apple launched the iPod, it swept away people's imagination of how a music device would look – it was so sleek and stylish, it could carry all their songs, and the size display, which was a big jump in those days, could show the album art. There is no better example than this device along with iTunes that changed the face of the music industry. It led the industry into a new era.

What is innovation?

At its simplest, innovation is about approaching a problem differently to find unconventional solutions.

A more relevant definition is that it's a consistent stream of initiates inspired by INSIGHTS to bring INCREMENTAL VALUE over time.

Innovation is often confused with an image of fancy outputs and cool companies. In the true sense, it's intelligent and out-of-the-box problem solving based on models and is applicable to even the minutest scale.

> *The example of Coke in the beverage industry shows how just **branding innovation** did the job for them. Coke constantly altered its message and branding with colours and fonts until they achieved that growth and market standing.*

| 1955 | 1963 | 1966 | 1970 | 1971 | 1976 | 1985 | 1989 | 1993 |

| 1994 | 1996 | 1997 | 1997 | 2000 | 2002 | current | summer '09 & '10 |

*Paint companies did similar innovation with packaging. It was started by a paint company called Dutch Boy, who realized the drawbacks of conventional buckets that paints used to be sold in and replaced those with jars that were easy to carry, easy to pour from and easy to seal back. This simple **innovation in packaging** put Dutch Boy in the front run.*

Innovation is also not limited to startups or struggling companies. It's a continual process that can lead companies/products/services

to keep up or take over the competitors. We spoke earlier about Google and how they constantly evolve to keep their game relevant.

Companies who do not evolve their products and offerings go into decline. Even the established products or companies, without innovation, get irrelevant with changing markets and thus cease to exist. Kodak is the perfect example.

5 Power Principles of Innovation

1. **Innovation is about insights, not ideas.**

    When looking at brainstorming sessions, the team is engaged in bringing lots of ideas to the table as thoughts or suggestions to a possible course of action. Ideas are important for the creative process, but there is a thin distinction here. There is no dearth of ideas to a problem, but what we need are good ideas. Those come from insights. Insights are the capacity to gain an accurate and deep understanding of something. Driving innovation is about ideas through insights. The better the insights are, the sharper is the approach to innovation.

    Uber is a great example of an insight-oriented idea that saw how there was a gap between customers and cab providers.

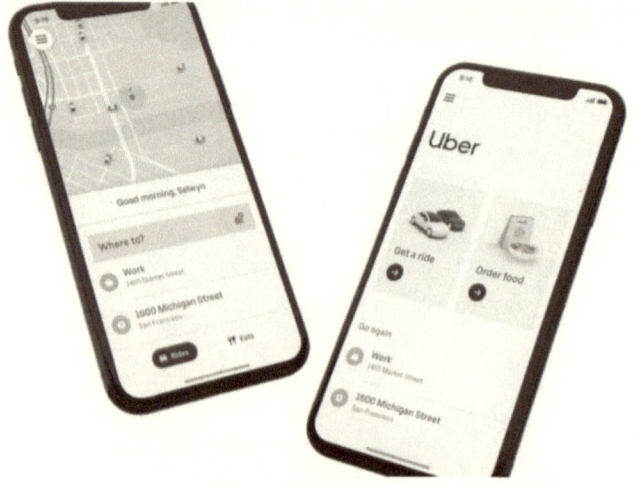

2. Innovation is about leading, not following.

Innovation needs to bring a phenomenal change from current market offerings in the customer experience or efficacy or both. Companies need to lead if they must create that shift in consumer behaviour. A marginal betterment is not good enough.

Apple undisputedly is a leader and its products have spearheaded in changing the behaviour of users through better experiences.

3. Innovation models are a set of theories based on studies, not random acts.

Innovations are based on theories that have been studied and developed by observations and precedence. Unlike common perception, they are not self-generating acts of random thoughts to create a bright idea. Each situation demands a specific model to be applied, and therefore executives must choose one or more theories for a particular situation, though innovation can be layered to get the right fit.

Like how a doctor would carefully choose from a battery of tests to arrive at his diagnosis, he would use one or more tests to correlate the results.

4. Innovation does not have limitation of scope.

Some innovations can be applied at a high level, like the assembly line process founded by Henry Ford, which radically changed manufacturing businesses and has been adopted from manufacturers as small as phones to as big as airplanes. Others can be micro innovations, like the bar scan system that is the basis of sorting parcels and airport luggage, without which modern airports cannot function.

5. Innovation does not have a scale.

Some innovations can lead to big businesses like Facebook. Others can be more niched business innovations like Epic Systems, who are in a very niche hospital management system and are disrupting their segment.

How you too can innovate

There are broadly three areas of innovation.

Product Innovation

This is the most known type of innovation that has to do with improvement of the physical product by reengineering and developing existing versions Product innovation also creates new lines of products.

Smartphones are a great example of product innovation.

Process Innovation

This is when a company chooses to change how they operate and innovate to gain efficiencies. It usually results in the application or introduction of a new technology or a method that helps organizations remain competitive and meet customer demands.

FedEx brings a promise of overnight delivery. How it achieves this through operations and management using a complex set of routing is a good example of process innovation. Swiggy is another example of a business completely based on process innovation.

Business Model Innovation

Business model innovation is mainly to do with how businesses conduct value transactions with their customers. It involves financial strategies and pricing innovations with the customers.

When Dell was launched, it was the first company to deliver computers to their customers directly and was seen as a great business model innovation.

Netflix is another example, who transformed the movie rental industry by using a subscription model combined with data analytics to provide a personal experience to users.

 Before moving forward, I would like you to identify the current status in your business from all the three areas and identify which part, when innovated, will deliver maximum impact.

Innovation when backed with strategy

Why do we hear about the companies whose products failed during their time, but today if we look back, we find them ahead of their time? There are several such examples in the aircraft and automobile manufacturing industries where, despite the product being highly evolved and innovative in its time, it didn't get that kind of sales.

So why is it that despite being innovative and being ahead of the curve, these products and companies did not get results? As it turns out, getting the innovation right is only one side of the coin, strategy being the other. Combined together into Strategic Innovation, it's what that gets the outcome.

Outcomes = Innovation + Strategy

Drawing from Sun Tzu's quote from 'The Art of War': "*Innovation without strategy is just noise. Strategy without innovation is a sure shot way to get extinct.*"

It is important that innovation efforts are focused at the right problem, right direction and on the right scale. Innovating in the wrong direction is equally bad as not innovating. The close relationship between the two is what keeps them in the right direction, and defines priorities and scale. Together, they bring meaning and create a step-by-step process to achieve outcomes.

Xerox company had a working model of what we know today as the user interface for personal computers in the late 1970s. They had innovated something that was about to change the computer industry and become the bedrock of modern computing.

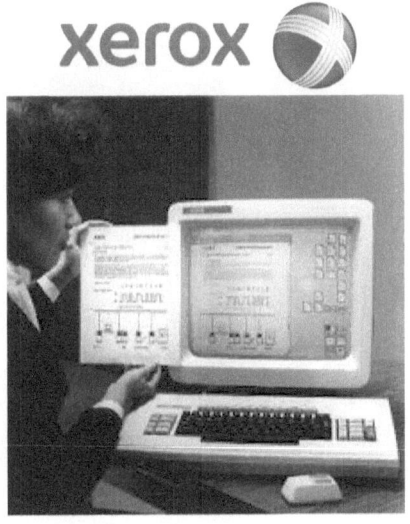

But it was Apple who took it forward after acquiring it from Xerox and they strategically innovated the concept into Macintosh. It won't be wrong to say that, if Apple had not bought the strategic outlook for the product, then the world would never have experienced a graphic interface in that manner.

The story does not end here.

Chapter 5

LEVELS OF IMPACT CREATED BY INNOVATION

Steve Job's philosophy for Apple products was about them being relentlessly beautiful and simple to use. The company kept innovating by rebuilding each version for more efficiency, better speed, beautiful design and increased ease of usage. What started as a user interface design of Macintosh developed further into offshoot programs like Pages, Key notes, Garage-band and Automator.

Simplicity and user friendliness inspired the development of iOS that became the platform for iPhones and later in iPad, and Apple kept on building more features in subsequent years. Later, Apple launched iCloud service that allowed users to keep files on cloud storage and access them through any of their devices. But the moment Apple launched App Store and allowed application development from third party developers, it opened a whole new way of using the iPhone and iPad.

For businesses and entrepreneurs, the meaning of portable digital and their possibility went on to another level. Companies began to develop specialty apps for their processes that they could run on the iPad. Automobiles, healthcare, space agencies, aircraft manufacturing - there is barely a sector that has not been touched by this revolution.

Notice how Apple kept on building block by block through a consecutive string of innovations. The first few gave the company a head start; later innovations added layers over layers until it reached the tipping point. The stage was set; all it required was one move, and what happened next changed the reality of portable digital as we had known.

* (Apple is being used as an example because it's familiar among most readers. There are other companies too that exist in niches that show similar impact.)

Innovation can be understood with four levels as illustrated in the diagram below. Using Circles of Transmutation™, we will take look at these impact stages on products, industries and consumers.

The first stage or the first impact is coping with cultural scape. Through these innovation, products and services tend to cope with cultural-scape, mostly to adjust into contextual reality. First impact

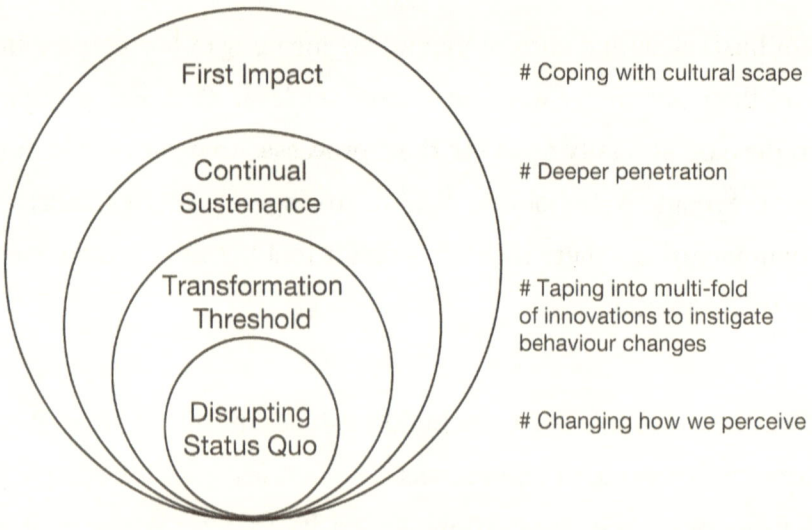

First Impact   # Coping with cultural scape

Continual Sustenance   # Deeper penetration

Transformation Threshold   # Taping into multi-fold of innovations to instigate behaviour changes

Disrupting Status Quo   # Changing how we perceive

sometimes is a significant step, because it lays groundwork for right course.

Continual sustenance are series of further innovations meant to challenge the contextual realities and achieve deeper penetration into the subject and market. When we start seeing behavioural changes as a result of these innovation, the impact now lies in the transformation threshold zone and is beginning to reforms trends.

Disrupting the status quo is the final level of impact where the meaning of product or services totally change and exceeds in perceived value.

Picking up from the story of the music industry, when the media changed from cassettes to CDs, we saw the first impact that greatly improved the quality of music. The next few years saw a continual

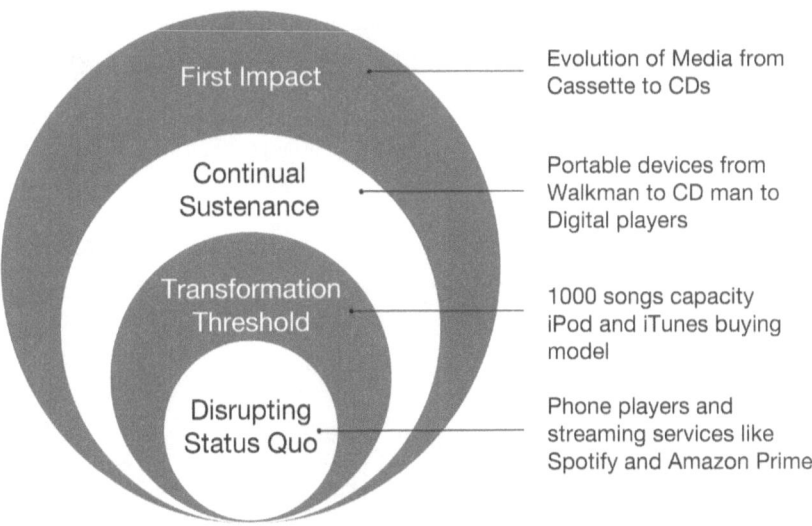

First Impact — Evolution of Media from Cassette to CDs

Continual Sustenance — Portable devices from Walkman to CD man to Digital players

Transformation Threshold — 1000 songs capacity iPod and iTunes buying model

Disrupting Status Quo — Phone players and streaming services like Spotify and Amazon Prime

sustenance phase with the development of CD players and other devices.

But it wasn't until digital tracks and players like the iPod came in that we began to see the tip of the iceberg. Further findings like iTunes - that changed how music was bought - added to the user experience. The final blow was seen with the release of smartphones capable of music players, streaming and an explosion of online music providers like online radio and Amazon Music. This is what disrupted the status quo.

 Try to map Apple's journey from facts as discussed above and see if you can identify each of the stages.

The most neglected principle of Innovation

The Sphere of Influence can be found across categories, in segments and companies. Its impact is not limited to scale, geography or era. However, there is a catalyst found behind every story of disruption and ironically, is the most subdued part of any conversation: VISION.

We spoke about how ideas lead to insights. It's the insights that lead to vision.

In the 1950s Japan was recovering from post-war damages and was trying to establish its infrastructure. Japanese industries were coming up in the areas of Osaka and Tokyo, creating a need to connect these two cities 500 kilometres (300 miles) apart, using a faster and more efficient system to meet the demand and for future expansion.

Japan adopted a solution that was not a popular one. During the same time, western countries saw air travel as the future and betted on larger planes, more airports and more connections. Japan decided to develop a high-speed rail line between these two cities. But it was going to be unlike any other railway ever known. A series of innovations were used to change the conventional rail logic into what the world would get to know as the 'bullet train'.

Project **Shinkansen** from its inception was a bold **vision.** It took an existing system and innovated it, transforming how it works. From train design, track construction, planning of routes, signalling methods, every aspect was re-looked at to meet the objectives, which were to make the trains go faster, and be safer and more efficient.

The project was looked at with scepticism from day one. Many critics thought that it was not wise to use an old system and create new routes through the mountainous terrain of Japan that required lots of tunnels and bridges. What made matters worse was that the budget, which had soared to almost double of the original estimate and was not considered economically viable. There were other concerns as well, like safety and limited number of tracks for high-speed trains only, which was using a different gauge then from Japan's other rail networks.

But the founders of this project believed in the vision and kept persevering. They had anticipated for growing demand over time and built the track to withstand massive capacities that would be required in future and that would make the project more than viable. They had also installed earthquake sensors of a new kind that would signal the train to stop and lock itself in case of tremors, a frequent phenomenon in Japan that made train travel unpopular in the first place.

Shinkansen opened in 1964 and reduced the travel time from six hours forty minutes to just under four hours. In the first three years itself, passenger numbers soared on this route, making the line one of the world's busiest. More than three hundred trains per side were carrying passengers within five years of its opening. Shinkansen became an icon of post-war recovery and placed Japan as the tech leader on the world map.

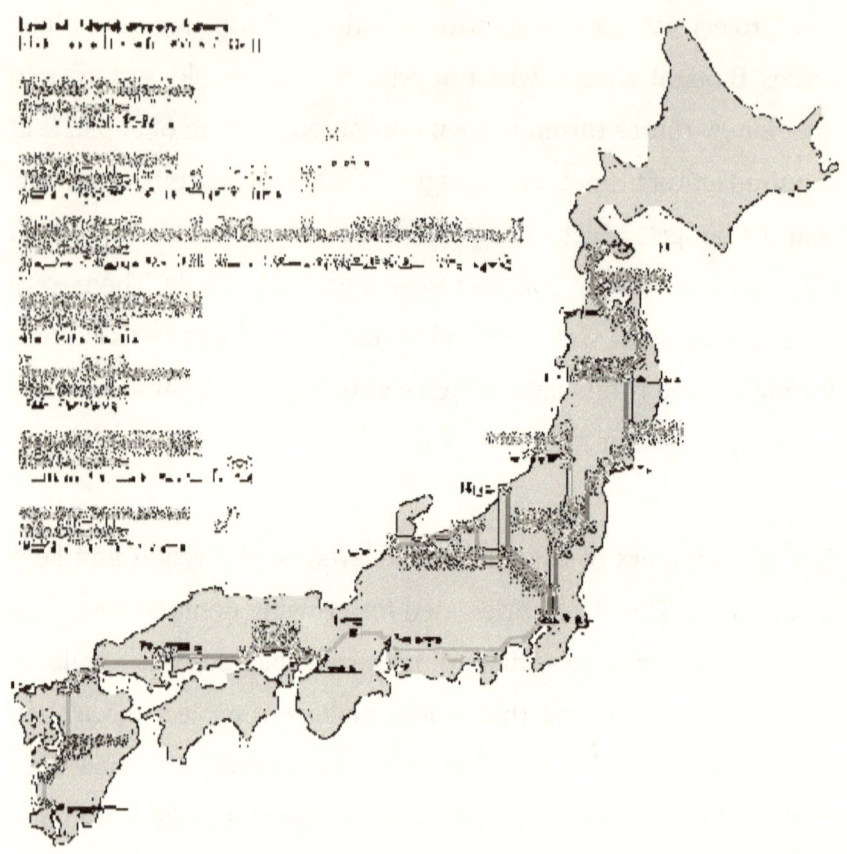

The original link was between Tokyo and Osaka. Since then, Shinkansen lines have connected the entire country from north to south.

(Source:http://blog.mailasail.com/beezneez/posts/2017/10/17/3945-first-bullet)

The Shinkansen project stacked up geography, technology and frequency of trains to create this impactful outcome.

Since then, in Japan, the Shinkansen network has been extended to connect the entire length of the country. Trains have been further developed for higher speeds and more efficiency. The Shinkansen network offered several advantages in Japan, including scheduling frequency and flexibility, punctual operation, comfortable seats, and convenient city-centre terminals.

Its feasibility was always compared to that of air travel. This can be further appreciated today, when Japan is struggling to find space to build new airports. Osaka Airport's new Kansai Airport has been built over reclaimed land. So these main airports are focused on international flights, and domestic transfers are largely being taken care of by the Shinkansen network.

In other parts of the world, high-speed rail networks picked up during the 1970s after seeing Shinkansen's success. Europe adopted high-speed rails for intercity connection. France's TGV and Germany's ICE trains spearheaded the reform.

One of the breakthroughs in Europe was the Euro tunnel project, a high-speed rail link beneath the sea that connected the island of the United Kingdom with mainland Europe. Never in history had these two geographical areas been connected before. High-speed rail now brought London, Paris, and Brussels closer to each other by Eurostar Rail.

In the United States of America, rail network was limited by the distances and found not feasible except for one geographical zone: the east coast. There are major cities like Boston, New York, Philadelphia, Baltimore, and Washington, DC located within close enough proximity for a rail network to effectively serve the area. Amtrak Corporation (a railway company) is innovating to lay groundwork to connect these cities by using high-speed railway.

Interestingly, a new, one of its kind, private train corridor is being planned and constructed in the state of Florida to connect Miami to cities in the north and extend all the way to Orlando. It caters to a niche that is too long for car and too short for a flight.

High-speed rail opened another niche possibility. Every major metropolitan area, regardless of where it is on the world map, is in need of bigger airports, and cities are running out of space. For expansion of airports, governments are compelled to look at the outskirts. But how do they connect them to the city?

High-speed railway was the obvious solution. We now find many airports outside the populated areas, which are connected to the city using high-speed networks. Shanghai Pudong, Beijing Daxing, Kuala Lumpur, Barcelona, London, Stansted and many more are such examples.

What started as a simple enough idea, innovated at various levels, has not only transformed the face of Japan's economy, but changed the way rail links are looked at.

That is the power of vision.

The vision of Shinkansen leaders changed the fate of railways. They exhibited three important attributes that got them to keep innovating:

- Optimism and faith
- Perseverance and determination
- Imagination and an eye for details.

Ironically, these are also the characteristics that are found in many good leaders and have been endorsed by business schools. So is it that good leadership disguises innovators?

We are going to discuss more about this in later chapters.

I would like you to take a break and go out to your favourite cafe. Take some white sheets with you and put your phone on silent. Write down your vision as if everything you are thinking can be achieved. There are no limitations for money, people, resources, connections or anything else. Dream and write everything that comes from your heart.

Chapter 6

NOW IT'S YOUR TIME TO 'DISRUPT'

It's fascinating to see how innovation can shape entire companies and industries. Like a seed, once planted and nurtured, it bears possibilities of limitless growth.

> *The big question is, how to do it? It is one thing to discuss and study success stories, but entirely another to innovate real-time. How does one get set on this journey?*

When I studied successful innovations and mapped out how they got there, I found patterns in their approach and context. I later developed this into practice - a three-stage road map is what I found is required to innovate. These are:

- **Gaining Awareness**
- **Making Choices**
- **Strategically Innovating.**

We will touch upon each of these phases to create a general sense of understanding. Since each company, segment, product and context is different, the method would have to be adjusted to suit individual scenarios.

Gaining Awareness

The awareness phase is about data gathering and gap finding for developing insights. What's working? What is not working? What needs to change? Where do we think the problem lies? Lots of questions and building an understanding is what this phase is all about.

Gaining awareness is the most powerful method that visionaries use that shapes their businesses. Successful companies are built around their awareness of the industry and the market.

- **Gaining awareness for an ESTABLISHED line of offerings**

  Existing lines are primarily dealing with improving or re-engineering for either efficiency or experience. Companies adopt market feedback, internal reviews and cues from their own experience. Awareness is about understanding or highlighting problems and creating a strategy around it. Here companies are adjusting the products to create a better version.

  When the detergent market was facing fierce competition, Surf Excel gained awareness that their product was hard on the hands. They discovered that by adding a hand softener and fragrance, they could greatly improve the experience of using their product. As a result, Surf Excel got a great boost in the coming years.

- **Awareness for NEW lines of offerings**

This is where awareness gets interesting. The paradox is that cues to new lines are also found in existing markets, but in a different way. Strategists, through their experience and surveys, try to find-out need gaps. They seek a very deep level of awareness looking for intangibles. They look where nobody is looking, they listen to what people are not saying. Need gaps are great opportunities to build businesses. Some of the most successful niches are born from here.

Let's take the example of Swiggy. The founders observed a major gap in the industry between restaurants and the consumers. A significant number of consumers needed food at home - an unsaid and uncaptured need. It was not until Swiggy used this gap to fill in did the industry realize that this gap existed. Swiggy's success is a direct result of pain awareness.

- **Awareness for SELF**

Awareness is incomplete without awareness about self. It is important to know about yourself as individuals and your company. Internal strengths, weaknesses, aspirations, flexibility are all part of strategy and therefore are part of the innovation process.

It's about being authentic as people and businesses, by finding the true reason behind a company's existence and nurturing that cause through innovation efforts.

- **Awareness for VISION**

Company goals and long-term vision play a huge role in defining micro steps in the innovation process. I have found in practice how vastly the direction changes from when we are aware about the long-term objective in contrast to when we are not. We are going to talk more about this in later chapters.

- **Awareness for PERCEPTIONS**

Companies need to know where they lie at each of these parts of the nested system: industry, category, segment, micro segment. Equally, it is required to understand the perception customers have about the system, the product and your company. How do they relate to the values you offer? Is it important enough for them or do they need something else?

Great niches are created when companies understand these.

- **Awareness of the fallacy of assumptions**

This is my favourite that dominates industries more than we realise. Basically, the system of organisation has standardised most of the phenomena by averaging, converting into simple numbers and making principal assumptions. It was done to ease out regular working, which it has.

But consider this, if one has to find the net worth of people in a small size unit, say an area in Seattle, one would certainly see the revenue index of that area and make a deduction. But for some reason, if the index area would also cover Bill Gate's residence, would the same averaging work? Obviously not. It was assumed while adopting the average that the bracket of income is similar.

Knowing assumptions is very important to get leverage during innovation. I have found that questioning the assumed has always led to new potential and openings.

How To Gain Awareness?

Yes, there are methods to the method! Let's see...

Methods for gaining awareness have evolved over time. More and more sophisticated tools and online research have helped gather data. By large, there are three ways to gain awareness.

Customer feedback/surveys

Most companies, especially B2C, go for customer feedback as their primary method to gain awareness - online surveys, feedback forms, behaviour analytics, etc. There are so many forms of feedback mechanism that help create essential insights.

In order for a survey/feedback to be effective, there are three primary components.

- First is **CONTEXT**. The survey must be set by understanding the culture, segment and user profile. Framing of questions must reflect this, and they may change for location or the segment.

- Second is **HYPOTHESIS**. What is the objective behind the survey? The queries and structure of the survey must lead towards this goal.

- Third is the **INTERPRETATION**. Most questions would not directly lead to the conclusion. Results must be abstracted using a certain methodology, by combining more than one answer and converged into more tangible output like percentiles or graphs.

There is a catch though; the reliability of feedback strategy depends on the questions being asked and the subject of investigation. More than 50% surveys don't reveal anything. One of the top factors is that the audience couldn't relate to the questions and thus did not invoke that kind of response.

The prevailing cultural belief system is another reason behind limited results.

> *Imagine a survey fifteen hundred years ago asking about centre of the universe. The result would surely have be the 'Earth'.*
>
> *Guess what it would have been five hundred years ago when asked about the shape of the Earth? 99.9% would have said flat.*

Cultural belief creates mass opinion. These kinds of feedbacks do not present any clear direction for businesses.

This brings us to the next point, how do you take a feedback for segments that do not exist?

> *What kind of survey led Steve Jobs to know that there would be a requirement for 10,000 songs in our pocket?*

Whiteboard canvas

Whiteboard canvases are 'do it yourself' exercises that use pre-set formats for steering thinking towards intended cause and discover ground. White board canvases are a great way to gain in-depth insights.

The biggest advantage of whiteboards is that it creates a pictorial representation of thoughts, findings and data using the canvases system. Research has found that the human cognitive mind finds data much easier to comprehend over vision and is able to process even complex problems when done visually.

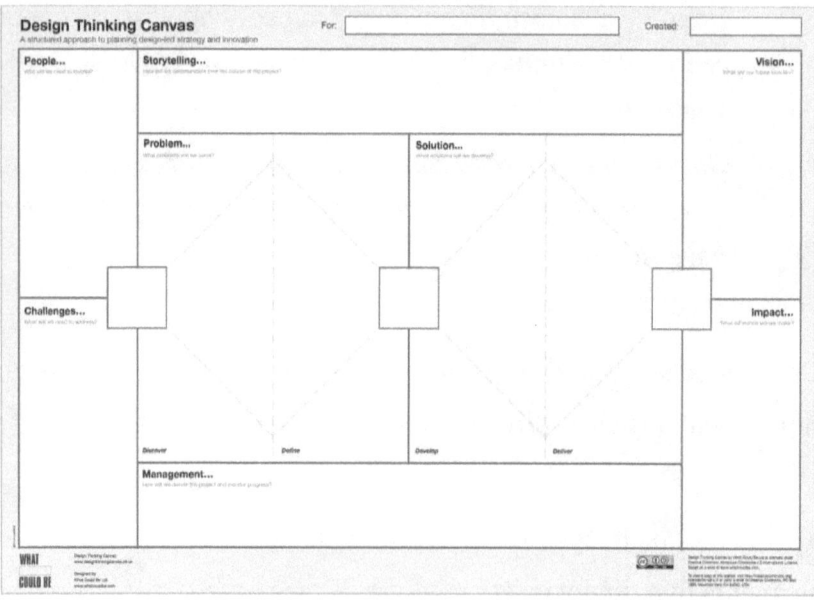

There are many DIY exercises that can be found from subject experts around the world on the web.

From innovation standpoints, there are some absolutely 'must do' whiteboard canvases that can be found on

www.utssavgupta.com/whiteboarddiy

For innovation discoveries, the core of whiteboard exercises is to arrange facets of business into modules. Starting from a common point, each business can thereafter develop a tailored structure suiting their niche.

As they progress, these structures also become an important part of the metrics of measurement that we are going to talk about in a later chapter.

When it comes to niche discovery, whiteboard exercises are the only way to find the hidden opportunities.

Whiteboard canvases are a great way to collaborate. Many companies also use them for internal brainstorming. But where it hits its limitation is due to a lack of further insights due to the same team and the same individuals.

The next leap in awareness comes not from the internal team, but from external collaboration. This method is called the 'Mastermind'.

Mastermind

Mastermind is a great strategy that has been emphasised by many business leaders and institutions. It is a group of entrepreneurs and experts, anywhere from two to twelve, with diverse backgrounds, who come together, discuss problems and give inputs.

Because of the group's collective acumen and a diversity of viewpoints, entrepreneurs achieve what otherwise would have been impossible to attain.

Mastermind works best when combined with other kinds of awareness models. I have seen Mastermind yielding phenomenal clarity and outstanding results when using the whiteboard structure

At my architectural company, conducting Mastermind sessions with our clients using Hepta-Interlinked system™ has brought incredible insights. This step alone has made such a huge difference in the design approach and its results as compare to a project started without mastermind.

Mastermind helped clients constitute a strong vision and enabled architecture to reflect that. These projects now stand as assets for the client organisation to stretch their wings for the next leap.

> *Mastermind combined with ODB™ created framework that led to bold designs behind some of the most prestigious projects at Creators Architects: the largest meditation centre of the world, the largest Vaishnav Spiritual complex of the world, a disruptive multi utility space for Delhi Technological University and more....*

The power of the mastermind is limitless and yields miraculous results when combined with whiteboard canvas structures. Napoleon Hill, in his book, 'Think and Grow Rich' has repeatedly emphasised the concept and to put it in use. Top business schools, in their curriculum, have also stressed on conducting frequent Masterminds.

This is the magic tool to develop new niches.

You can learn more about Mastermind on

www.utssavgupta.com/mastermind

To take a pilot of Mastermind for problem solving with your internal teams, just to write us at: mastermind@utssavgupta.com.

You can be a part of a Mastermind group composed of entrepreneurs.

 What aspects do you need more awareness on? Write down what comes to your mind immediately, and in a separate column write down what you know for sure is right.

Making Choices

After gaining information, the next step is to develop a strategic road map for channelling the process. It's about making choices to narrow it down to one or a few options to take your efforts forward.

The trick is in making smart and clear choices for the most favourable direction. Like a sharpshooter who carefully chooses the targets and acts with precision.

Making choices is the most important and is also the hardest part. One can look at choice making in a couple of ways.

- **Sequencing**

Sequencing choices based on logical, chronological order.

- **Priority**

Choosing based on the order of priority.

- **Low-hanging fruits**

Catching the easy-to-do things first.

- **Immediate relief**

Choosing based on what would bring immediate results.

- **Filtering out less productive avenues**

Killing some options to focus more on others.

> *Google has a spring clean-up session every year to trim down its research and choose to focus on a few potential streams. This is one of the reasons why Google products are sharp and innovative.*

Creating the Domino Effect

This method is my personal favourite.

Ever heard the phase 'falling dominos'? Imagine bicycles in the parking lot standing side by side closely. A person knocks the first one and it begins to fall. It pushes the second cycle and that too starts to fall. The second one falls on to the third, pushing it to fall, and before we know it, all the bicycles are in a cascade effect and they all fall.

This is called the domino effect. When one push creates enough momentum to self-induce force in the entire system. What's even better is that the domino effect works just as effectively if the objects are bigger than the one before.

It's like a small rock rolling from the top of a mountain that hits the bigger one below. The bigger rock starts rolling and hits an even bigger one, and so the cycle continues.

The domino effect is a very effective strategy where choice is made based on what will set the ball rolling. It's about which piece to focus on first that will create a chain reaction effect for the others.

It is interesting to note that the domino effect is also a war strategy. Both parties try to find weak spots that will create a domino effect. It is also used by psychologists to treat their patients.

Write down your goals, one each, on a yellow sticky pad slip and put them on your workspace whiteboard. Now rearrange them sequentially in the manner of progression and see if it works like dominos.

Choosing where to innovate

There can be many kinds of innovation and areas of application. From the examples cited in the previous chapters, we have seen how companies have innovated on processes, branding, packaging and even on their complete product line.

When we are setting a strategic objective, choosing which areas to innovate is driven by the intended result.

> *United Parel Service, one of the three largest logistics company in the Unites States, wanted to increase their efficiency. They looked at various options where the company could have innovated: faster connection, better software, more frequencies of connections. In the end, they chose to innovate at the delivery level, which was the last link. They developed a route planning system that utilised maximum signal-free turns to navigate their vehicle. This way, the new routes increased their fuel efficiency and decreased delivery timing by 15%.*

Quite an unconventional choice, don't you think? One would never think of innovation at the delivery level making such dramatic impact.

Chapter 7

STRATEGICALLY INNOVATE

This is where rubber meets the road.

After carefully identifying areas to innovate, the next step is to perform quick iterations for each layer to assess possible scope and impact level using a process called Design Sprint. We talk more about this on www.**utssavgupta.com**

Like how every lock has a specific key, every goal has a particular kind of innovation that would unlock the problem. Innovation models are based on theories, each theory based on a set of principles, and thus it is required to see what theory to apply in a specific context.

Stacking layers of innovation interventions is what creates massive impact, like how it happened in the music industry and with Shinkansen. The persistent and coherent approach of a string of innovations that are well-aimed and well-timed is what creates disruption.

Jobs to be done

It is commonly believed that the user is the primary cause for buying any products or services. Companies focus their entire research on consumer understanding in order to develop the product. But, here is a thought:

> *Mr. Patel is an entrepreneur who is in the business of financial services. He is well into his forties, has two kids, lives in an apartment, drives to work and likes to travel as a hobby. However, none of these attributes causes him to buy the 'Forbes' magazine that he purchases every month.*

> *As it happens, the physical attributes of Mr. Patel did not cause him to buy the products, which in this case is 'Forbes' magazine, which he reads to keep himself updated with the business world.*

> **It was a JOB he was trying to do.**

When we buy products, we essentially 'hire' them in order to help us do a certain job. If the product does the job well, then we tend to hire the product again. And if it does a substandard job, we tend to 'fire' it and look for an alternative.

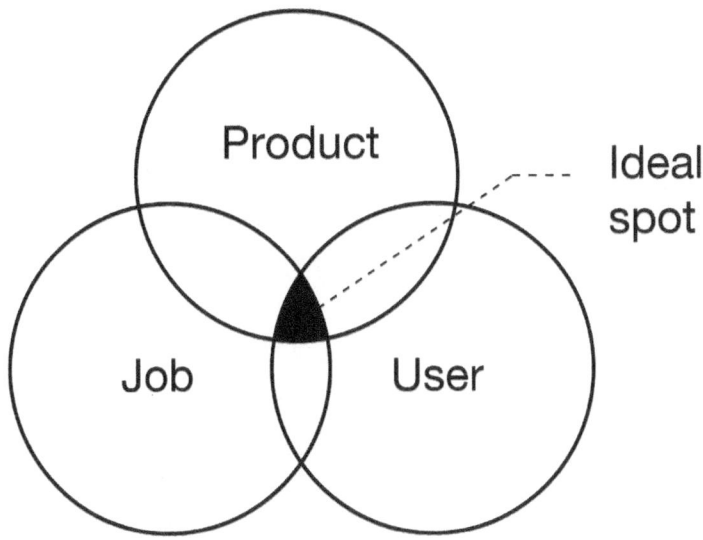

The 'jobs to be done' theory is about focusing on the job rather than the customer and developing products/services to complete the job.

Theodore Levitt, an American economist and a professor at the Harvard Business School, was editor of the 'Harvard Business Review'. He used to tell his students:

> *"People don't want to buy a quarter-inch drill. They want a quarter-inch hole!"*

There is the famous milkshake research that highlighted the theory real-time and brought it centre stage:

> McDonalds wanted to understand how to improve sales of their milkshake product and commissioned an extensive research. They took feedback and incorporated the response like making shakes chocolatier, chunkier, playing with sizes, etc. These changes made no effect on the sales. McDonalds thereafter made many efforts, but they too did not lead to any result. Only when researchers started asking the' job' consumers were trying to get done by 'hiring milk shakes', did they get their answers of what would drive sales.

Uber is based on the jobs-to-be-done model.

> Uber realised that customers need to hire a car every now and then in the most efficient manner. At the same time, car drivers were also looking for customers. Uber connected the Users and Car Drivers to get their job done.

Successful companies segment their products based on 'jobs' for specific customer segments, not the other way round.

> Boeing and Airbus, for example, create their planes for distinctive segments based on particular jobs airlines are

trying to get. Some companies have even built products catering to more than one job and thus achieve diversity through this mechanism.

Understanding 'The JOB'

Make no mistakes, this is one of the trickiest parts of innovation. Don't worry, we have made it simple for you.

Understanding the 'JOB' that the user really wants and would motivate him or her to buy the product or services, comes from the awareness exercises that we discussed in Chapter 6 using the JTBD framework below..

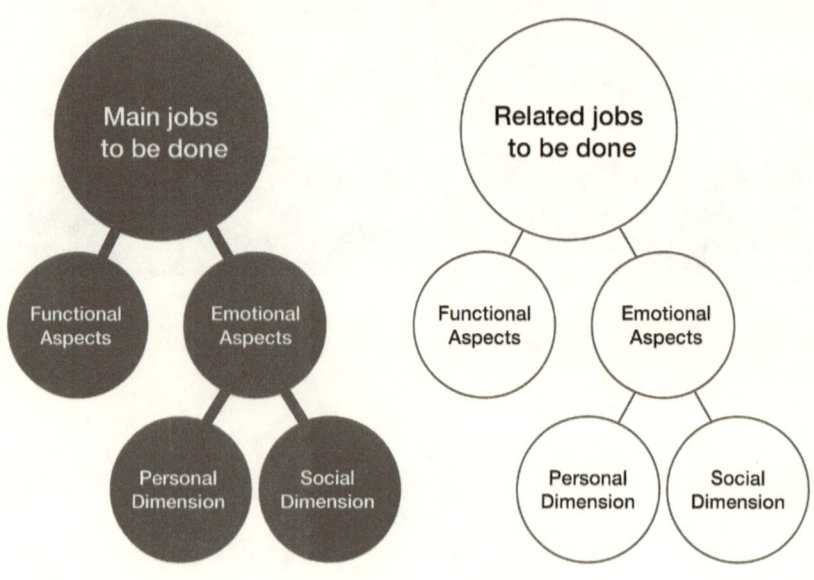

The Job has primarily two dimensions. First is the functional aspect - that is the physical purpose the user is trying to get done.

A customer buys airline services for purpose of travelling from one city to the other in the most efficient manner. It is because of this job that international airlines that serve transcontinental routes, take huge effort in getting the flight scheduling right and minimise airport waiting time. Their popularity greatly depends on how smooth the connections are.

The second dimension is about the emotional needs of the user on personal and social dimensions.

Expanding on the same example, budget airlines provide a limited experience and curtail on-board food, baggage allowance, etc. On the other hand, a full-service airline goes an additional mile to render their services for passenger comfort, taking care of the minutest details. These two segments exist to serve a different job on an emotional level.

Let's look at the example of Uber from this perceptive.

Uber's functional job was to connect the passenger with car drivers for point-to-point transportation. In the conventional method, they would have set up a call centre for passengers to call and book their cabs. But Uber found that not only did the passengers want to book their cabs, they wanted to do so in the easiest, most minimalist and most seamless manner while staying fully informed about the cab's whereabouts. Hence live updates were developed, and the GPS locator allowed both parties to know their location, making the whole process seamless. This was the emotional need met by the Uber app.

At some point, safety was also a rising concern. So Uber built in security features in the app like reviews, call for help, tracking, etc., while the car was carrying the passenger.

Uber's success is attributed to how well they understood the JOB on both the dimensions.

But how did Uber ever acquire such detail for the job? What mechanism can companies follow to understand what the customer is really trying to achieve?

We will discuss this in the next section.

Building resilience through JTBD

The jobs-to-be-done theory focuses on the 'job' as a starting point. However, it is not set restricted to just one job, allowing innovators to look at a wider set around the core job.

By catering to more than one job or 'related jobs', companies diversify their 'risks'. This is especially a beneficial strategy for developing high investment ultra-niche products or processes such as aircrafts, supply chains or building projects.

> **Assessing risks and managing them through JTBD helps innovators build RESILIENCE. By doing so, it radically increases the value of the solution while lowering their risks.**

Interestingly, the benefits of resilience building are not only limited to providing increased value. Within the nested system, when is resilience developed at each layers, it changes economies sustainability and helps stabilise the entire ecosystem.

This is what saved companies and countries during major economic crisis and epidemics.

Case study: World Heartfulness Centre

Let me now share the story behind the World's Largest Meditation Centre designed by my company Creators Architects. Using this example, we shall illustrate how the jobs theory shaped the concept.

Our clients required a space where about fifty thousand plus people could sit together and meditate during their celebrations, which happened four times in a year lasting for three days each.

The most obvious way to look at it was to create a big seating arena and cover it from the top. Essentially, it would have created one big shed of 300m in both directions. It would roughly be even bigger than large airport terminal buildings.

As exciting as the scale was, when we started looking at the case using the Jobs theory, we found that it was not only about seating people but creating a peaceful experiential environment.

> *Requoting Theodore Levitt here, "People don't want to buy a quarter-inch drill. They want a quarter-inch hole!"*

Analysing the strategy using the JTBD framework to meet the design case, we found several factors that were not contributing towards the desired outcome. In other words, what seemed like a straightforward solution, when expanded on the nitty-gritties of functional and emotional dimensions, did not help in serving the job.

The microclimate of the space with fifty thousand people sitting just would not create conditions for a period of long seating, especially when there is no air conditioning. In addition to that, the movement patterns of whole space were very heavy and congested.

> *Through further analysis, we started focusing on the related job as well and started investigating what the job of the space was during the rest of the days when celebrations were not happening.*

These findings completely changed the concept. The organisation regularly conducted trainings of various sizes through the year. So instead of a central scheme, if we were to adopt a scheme that was de-centralised, i.e. small halls around the main hall, not only would it provide space for other trainings and activities, it would also solve most of the critical problems of the central scheme.

- Due to smaller halls, micro-climate and movement could be better controlled.

- It would offer multiple smaller spaces to conduct trainings.

- It would create an open space in the centre and, with landscape, it would create smaller spaces for seekers to explore.

- It would create an exploratory experience within the campus.

- Steps and open spaces would act like an amphitheatre space to hold information gatherings.

- These ancillary spaces would provide extra spaces for expansion and accommodate more people during meditations.

Insights got from 'Jobs to be Done' shaped the design and it went ahead to become the world's largest meditation centre, which now can house seventy thousand people in formal spaces and hundred thousand people overall.

To read more about World Heartfulness Centre, visit http://www.creatorsarchitects.com/works-hfn-meditation-hall-hyderabad.php

Empathy design

Don't get confused with big words like empathy. It simply means understanding the customers by getting into their shoes.

Empathic design is a user-centred design approach that pays attention to the user's feelings towards a product. In this process, we bring the user to the centre of the process and develop an understanding about them through empathy.

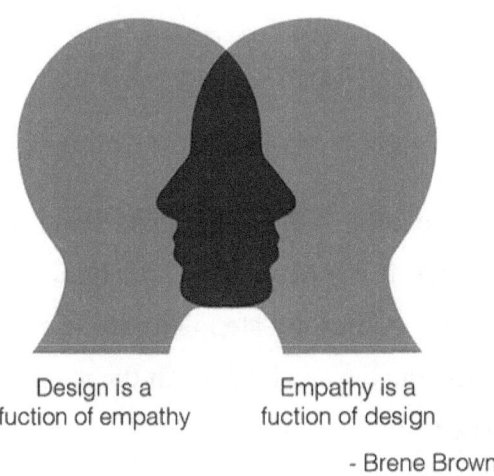

Design is a
fuction of empathy

Empathy is a
fuction of design

- Brene Brown

Questions like why, how, what, etc, are asked to gather and map as much information as possible, including the customer journey, pain points, their experience, etc. The primary objective is to bridge the gap of what the customer feels and what products deliver, to get a more experiential value.

Intuitive user interface is a great example of empathy design. Development of service industries, especially in healthcare, have adopted this kind of innovation, and now we see patient-centric facilities like Cleveland Clinic and Mercy.

Make my trip is another example that transformed transparency levels and offered choices to customers.

There is a thin line here. While 'Jobs to be Done' is the umbrella theory that defines the function and emotion, empathy design focuses on user experience by stepping into users' shoes to find out how smoothly the job can be done in the most human centred way. They are two sides of the same coin.

Empathy design has taken user experience to the next level. Even within competitors, it is the interphase of companies and how they interact with their customers that have come out to make such a difference for companies' standing and their competitive edge.

Why would some consumers prefer iOS and are not able to switch to Android, and vice-vera? Don't we all have a few favourites like between Swiggy or Zomato, Ola or Uber, Amazon or Flipkart, all based on how comfortable we are with their interphase?

This is the reason companies invest in improving their websites and applications year on year. New fields such as user experience (UX design) have emerged as a result, which are not dedicatedly working towards how users interact with websites and other digital media.

We shall discuss more about front-end interphase and how companies can retain customers' loyalty in further programs on **www.utssavgupta.com.**

 Interview your top five customers and take feedback on what experiences they had using your products or services. Use the power of questions and change them based on individual personalities as per what we had discussed in Chapter 6.

Case Study: Apex Hospital

We will illustrate further the concept of empathy design using another project: Apex Hospital, Jaipur.

Hospitals are the most stressful, daunting and scary experiences for patients and their family. There is fear of the unknown and fear about consequences, coupled with anxiousness and hope.

It is an equally emotionally stressful environment for doctors and nurses. This is how the profession is.

Our clients were dedicated to change this experience using processes, clarity and infrastructure to make the entire journey better.

> **We were looking to create a 'USER-CENTRIC' environment that not only 'PERFORMS' for efficiency through process improvement, but also caters to the emotional wellbeing of patients, attendants, doctors, nurses and other people working.**

As brilliant as the vision was, it was also very tricky. How to weave the emotions of people of such diverse nature into such a technically driven building that has so many complexities and compliances?

The answer came from innovation by empathy design. Innovation by empathy guided the entire design process, creating niches for each user kind and weaving it closely with functional aspects of the buildings.

Empathy design guided the function program for user centric spaces and created ethical guidelines that translated in home-like rooms, vibrant ICU design, relatable and assertive facade design, resting spaces, more use of natural light, development of central greens, etc.

Read more about Apex Hospital at: http://www.creatorsarchitects.com/works-apex-hospital-jaipur.php

Develop niches: The answers lie in the New Found Zone

Ever wondered about the secret behind those companies who have disrupted markets?

They developed niches that no other company could beat. In other words, they created an uncontested space for themselves and offered unparalleled values.

> *Southwest Airlines found a market space that was low cost and yet provided a cheerful experience for the traveller. They went on to become the most successful airline in the US market, owning the third largest market share in terms of revenue and highest by passenger count.*

How did Southwest crack this?

When we look at the way conventional industry works, companies belong to specific segments boxed in their own values. They would make them in extremities.

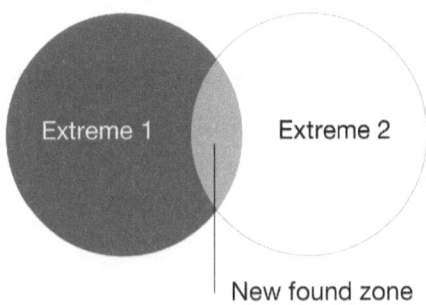

New found zone

Going back to the airlines industry, either there would be low-cost airlines, which would provide cheap tickets but no experience, or full-service airlines with good experience but expensive tickets.

The new found zone is a hidden zone that is reached through value reengineering and innovating for those values that are desirable to the customers.

Southwest Airlines found the new found zone for themselves and innovated to provide the experience of full-service airlines and the cost structure of low-cost airlines. Or course, they could not have all the aspects of the full-service segment and all of those of the low-cost segment. They carefully selected values for each segment that mattered to the customers.

In this way, Southwest found a new niche. Finding the new found zone is a strategy that other businesses from different industries have also used.

> *In the car industry, developers at Hyundai took a similar approach while developing Creta. They created a segment of mini SUVs, giving consumers the experience of SUVs for the price of regular cars.*

Creta unlocked the new found zone where competition did not exist.

Case Study: Raj Soin Hall

In another case study from Creators Architects, Raj Soin Hall for Delhi Technological University, a prestigious institution in the capital city, illustrated how we can find niches in new found zone.

The client required a multi-utility hall in their campus that could house three thousand people, to be used for various actives, but especially for convocation.

The design used innovation through 'Jobs to be done' and the new found zone.

On one extreme was a flat hall arrangement with a large cover on the top. This would have restricted the view of the stage due to the large dimensions of the space. The other extreme option was an auditorium seating arrangement. Had that been adopted, the space could not have been used for any other purpose.

The solution was in finding the new found zone, with half flat and half stepped seating that provided a perfect opportunity to use the flat area for various actives including ballet, sports, huddles, collaboration, etc. The other half provided perfect line of sight to the stage in full seating capacity and could accommodate half capacity symposiums. It even provided space below the stepped seating for other facilities like a cafeteria, toilets and offices.

Innovation by finding the new found zone also drives technical design aspects like acoustics, lighting and air conditioning. Instead of using conventional methods, an incremental method was used for air ventilation that took care of the indoor air quality and reduced electrical loads by a steep margin.

The design of Raj Soin Hall is a perfect example of designing for the new found zone to innovate.

To read more about Raj Soin Hall, please visit: www.creatorsarchitects.com/works-dtu-raj-soin-hall.php

Start with a Problem that you want to solve

As the late Steve jobs used to say to his team, *"You gotta find a problem that you like to solve, a wrong that you want to make right. You must be passionate about it, otherwise you won't have the perseverance to see it through."*

Great innovations come from the strategy of solving problems. It is not limited to an existing industry like search engines where Google believed in a better way to do the job and innovated towards it, or a new unfound industry, like in the case of Airbnb.

Airbnb found a problem and it tapped into the market of homeowners having spare rooms that they would like to provide for guests to stay and therefore generate revenue. At the same time, the travellers' segment that preferred to stay in boutique and experiential properties rather than standard hotels was growing. Airbnb saw this problem and created a business model around it.

At the same time, OYO in India was addressing a different problem.

OYO saw the problem of guesthouses with a few rooms always being left out. OYO built its business model by taking several left-out rooms in each property and offering them at flat pricing to potential customers who were looking for basic facilities. OYO unlocked a new model of business delivery for the guesthouse owners and catered to a new segment of customers.

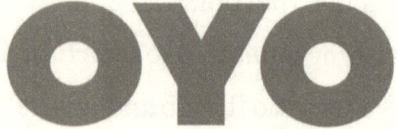

It is fascinating to see how innovation for problem solving is also not limited to scale and scope. It can start at a most basic level.

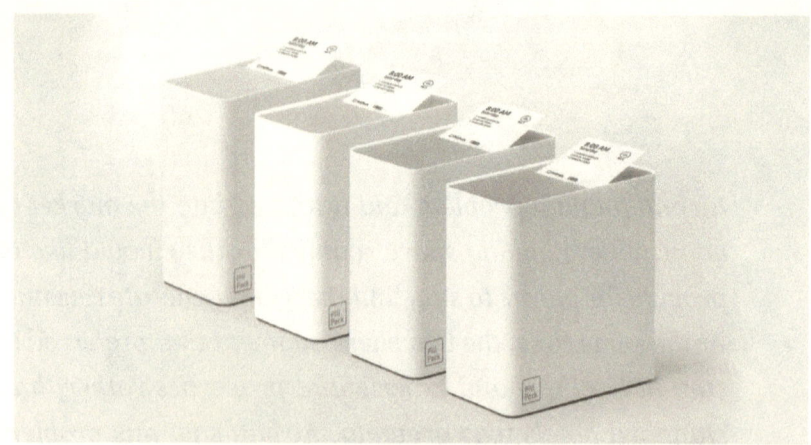

The founders of Pill Pack found that managing medicines was notoriously hard. There were a lot of pills that needed to be taken in various combinations throughout the day. Carrying entire strips of medicines was bulky, unmanageable, and often led to errors. Existing solutions like medicine manager were also dependent on the person doing so and how well he can read the prescription against the medicines' names. Either way, it was very time consuming and not error proof. Pill Pack picked up this problem and innovated on how medicines should be packed. Customers could now upload their prescriptions on their website, and pharmacists would pack the medicines as per each dose and put them in individual packs. As a result, consumers need only open a pack when it is time to have the medicine to take it.

Once again, Pill Pack betted on a combination of user convenience, problem solving and front-end interphase to develop their niche. Stacking of innovation models is once again clearly visible in their approach.

Now we are going to take a break from innovation models discussion. My intention is to get you started in the process of innovation. So far the concepts discussed will provide essential building blocks to get the ball rolling.

Don't worry, if you want to learn more, I have included more innovations models as part of advance program on

www.utssavgupta.com

Chapter 8

TAKING THE NEXT LEAP

PHEW... finally we have arrived at the last part of the book.

I hope you have got valuable insights so far and finding innovation not as daunting as it may have appeared before you picked up this book.

It is actually quite simple: one just needs to have a positive outlook towards it. Let me share one of my favourite stories - the comeback of Nokia.

Nokia, a Finish company, was dominating the mobile device market. Nokia devices were found in every part of the world and appealed to every segment of customers. It was one of the most popular and recognised brands of the time. In 2008, the launch of the iPhone followed by Android OS rapidly changed the device market.

Nokia took a serious hit in market share and could not retain its market dominance. As a result, the company spiralled down so fast that, in 2012, it was on the verge of bankruptcy.

The new Chairman of the board and CEO of Nokia joined in 2012 and started working on a strategical shift of the company's direction. They dropped the devices business and focused on the networking business. Changes were also made in the company board and leadership positions to reinstate a positive culture.

As a result, Nokia bounced back as a solid brand, the same as it used to be, in a new segment. It did not lose its core or its mission of 'connecting people'.

In this story, out of all the modern strategies and tactics Nokia applied, the most important one was relentless, paranoid optimism.

The downfall of Nokia was not due to a managerial decision in the conventional sense, but as it happens, most companies that have ceased to exist underwent a similar phenomenon.

Developing Culture

Nokia instilled a powerful sense of positivity, which started changing their paradigm, resulting in a culture of growth.

It is the underlying culture in businesses that motivates people and creates results. All innovative companies have a strong foundation of 'culture'. Further, using mission statements, companies align teams towards common goals.

National Aeronautical and Space Agency (NASA) is a premier organisation that has been into deep space exploration for the longest time. I would like to cite one of their mission statements from the Apollo XIII program.

"Failure is not an option."

NASA missions face unknown challenges that are dangerous to human life and research. Even the existing technology and materials fall short of meeting these challenges. So, how do they deal with such unfathomable situations?

NASA has instilled a culture of innovation and perseverance. Their team has a deep sense of commitment towards the cause, and as an organisation, they have set up metrics to drive the efforts.

This creates a self-drive within teams and leadership that pushed ideas to the edge in search of something new. There are numerous movies on space exploration where the directors have captured problem solving in NASA and how technicians, astronauts, ground staff, leadership... everyone is committed to solve the problem.

In certain ways, Nokia and NASA had many things in common. They both clearly developed a culture of positivity and perseverance. However, the key difference between these two is that Nokia developed this culture when things were at an all-time low. For NASA, their high-risk nature of missions and continual building up has been the instigator.

On the other hand, there are many established companies who are trying to innovate. However, their prevailing culture, which is working very well for them for their existing line of work, seldom supports the necessary agility required for innovation to happen. In this paradoxical dilemma, it does not make sense for leaders to change the culture, nor can they sustain without innovation.

> *So what do companies and their leaders do? How can they still bring a culture of innovation without changing the existing?*

There is another way: by setting up a special purpose vehicle. The strategy is to create a separate entity or a body, possibly within the existing company, that is independent and thus is free from the limitations that were stopping innovation.

Later, this strategy became what we now know as 'START-UPS'.

The advantage of setting up these independent bodies is that the culture and system can be specifically designed to achieve the mission objectives and, therefore, would be extremely focused and efficient.

In the Shinkansen example discussed earlier, the project was set up as a special purpose vehicle with a specific aim and objective. Southwest Airlines began like a start-up with a clear target segment.

We will talk more about 'start-ups' and how to develop them at **www.utssavgupta.com**

Taking the next step now means setting up a culture that instigates response, response results in action, action requires strategy, and strategy requires a way to measure.

Measuring Success

This topic I believe is one of the core fundamental and requires elaborate that is not possible to cover in this book. However, due to its importance, I felt compelled to write about it here in shorter form.

> **One of the great debates of the modern world has been about how to measure success. What are the right metrics to follow? What should be really measured in organisations, which would represent true results?**

As it happens, this is also one of the top reasons for why companies fall. It limits innovation due to the way they measure outcomes and eventually how they drive decision making.

Modern finance structures are based on ratios like ROI, IRR and other kinds of financial representations. In order to increase profitability, investors and corporations wish to reduce time and focus on those innovations that yield the fastest profitability.

The pursuit of fast profitability promotes only efficiency-based innovations and thus misses out on the kind that provides long-term disruption. This phenomenon is shaping companies, industries and even countries. Japan is a great example of an efficient innovations producer of the twenty-first century. One hardly sees disruptive innovation coming out when only a few decades ago, many disruptive innovation companies like Sony and Toyota originated from the same country.

Prof. Clayton Christensen's works explain in great depth on this subject and the impact it has had on innovation choices, thus on economies.

'Harvard Business Review' came out with a journal dedicated to Metrics in October 2019, talking about number-driven strategies.

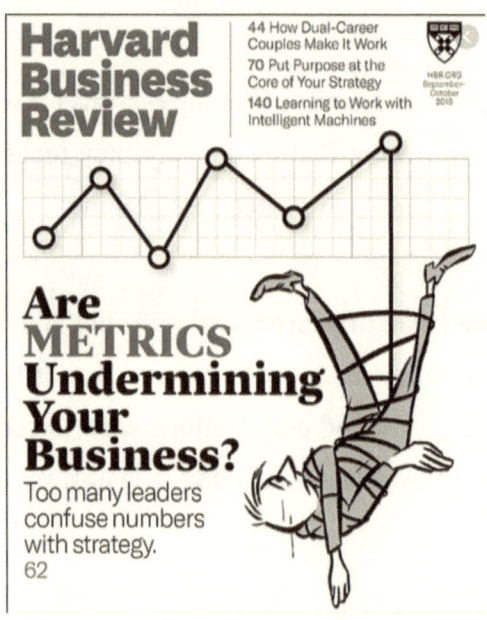

It is surprising to see how a vast majority of companies are following the conventional metrics. Interestingly innovative companies like the ones we have discussed about in this book have a different kind of system which is also the reason for their difference in decision making and their unique direction.

Model driven metrics

NASA has a clear objective and they are driven by their mission. So was Nokia, for their mission to connect people. Companies who set clear objectives and set a process to measure their steps towards those objectives get better results.

> *Intel and Google use an OKR framework to measure their direction. When Chrome OS was being developed, Sundar Pichai, CEO of Google LLC, was head of the program for Chrome development. He set an objective to do so and chose to measure it based on the number of users.*

In this example, their innovation efforts were clearly geared up towards building more user-centric features to gain more preferability among users.

Setting the right framework for innovation using methods, discussed in Chapter 6, is further supported by the right culture, decision making and appropriate goals, tracked with goal-oriented metrics. This is what differentiates a good Strategic Innovation from short-term progress.

How can you develop a metrics program for your business?

Remember about Gaining Awareness from an earlier chapter? Start with Whiteboard DIY and explore what parameters can be measured. Validate it with your Mastermind group. Make sure that you include the areas that matter to the growth of your company.

The fastest way to generate metrics is to use the same criteria that were used to create the innovation.

At Creators Architects, during the predesign phase, we use the Hepta-Interlinked System™ to capture the business case for clients and initial briefs. It's a six-axis framework that allows us to take an in-depth stock of the situation. Later, during design development, we found the effectiveness of the Hepta-Interlinked System™ for measuring how far we have reached our aims. So, the basis of creation also became the basis of metrics.

We will cover more about this metrics in the advanced program on www.utssavgupta.com

 What drivers do you currently use to inform your business? Are they only sales and revenue? Do they reflect your vision and goals, which you found in earlier exercises?

Building Resilience

As I was in the finishing stages of this book, a lockdown came into effect due to the Covid-19 global pandemic. There was great fear and panic in the country. Businesses had shut down, the economy was slowing down, and entrepreneurs were worried about how to manage during this period.

A few members of a group asked me to take a webinar on how organisations can innovate for such times. It was then that I realised the importance of this subject and chose to include a small part of it in the book.

The Covid-19 pandemic is considered to be a 'BLACK SWAN EVENT', the kind that is very unlikely to happen but would have severe consequences when it does. The impact includes a complete disruption in supply chains, nose diving stock markets and a shortage of many supplies.

So what does one do in such a case?

Let's shift our lenses for a moment and look at it from a different perspective. Disruptions similar to that from Back Swan events happen more often that we realise. The COVID pandemic is, of course, the most severe of all. However, the Ebola epidemic in

2014, the 2008 global economic crash, the 2000 World Trade Centre attack, and many more have yielded similar results.

Disruption for businesses are also caused at regional levels, like due policy changes, tax introductions, sector restrictions, local epidemics, etc. Even personal level catastrophes and accidents create disruption for organisations.

> *So, is being future ready only about pandemics and crises of any level?*
>
> *Or is future casting a purpose of every organisation as a part of evolution?*

One of the solution to this lies in Building Resilience.

It is to be proactive rather than reactive and create resilient mechanisms in your organisations that can sustain through such low periods. It's about how we look at our risks, especially the silent ones, and rearrange the entire eco system based on resilience as a goal.

Read more on risk as a part of planning framework: The Hepta-Interlinked System™ *on www.*utssavgupta.com

Building resilience shall no longer be a choice. COVID-19 will fuel the next wave of business and innovation.

Watch the complete webinar on:

www.utssavgupta.com/futurecasting-beyond-covid

 Using the concepts discussed in this book and awareness exercises, identify the silent risks and how for building resilience in your organisation. Jot them down in a table format with two columns saying risks and mitigation strategy. Send your findings to me on ug@utssavgupta.com

CONCLUSION

Before putting my pen down, I would like to thank you for taking out time to read this book. I hope it will help you to get the Rebound in your business.

If I were to sum up the concepts talked about in the book into the most important takeaways, they would be:

1. Innovation leads to unimaginable growth that leads to money.

2. Innovation combined with strategic moves is the best way towards outcomes.

3. What has worked for you in the past will not always work for you in the future unless you cultivate a culture of innovation.

4. Companies who drive strategic innovation based on Vision and not short-term numbers are more likely to succeed and be around for a while.

5. Efforts based on just luck are the quickest way to get extinct.

6. Innovation is a constant process and can even render competition irrelevant.

7. Layering and staking of the right innovation efforts can disrupt companies, segments and even industries.

If you have any more queries or clarifications, you may write to me at my personal email id: ug@utssavgupta.com

I am usually very prompt on email, but in case I am traveling, it may take a little more time to get back.

There are plenty of resources that you can download, and more are constantly added. You may subscribe to receive the latest workings on www.utssavgupta.com

I would encourage you to read this book again and start making notes of thoughts as they flow. Use this book as a guide for your innovation process.

Research has proven that we can rewire the neuron path through repetition.

A pre-recorded audio copy of this book is available as a download, exclusively for the owners of this book, at www.utssavgupta.com/ rebound

Wishing you the very best.

Thank you.

About the Author

Utssav Gupta is an Innovation Catalyst and founder of Black Swan Lab, where he focuses on distinct industry problems and their vision, to find an alternative approach models through innovation. He is an architect by education and is CEO/partner at Creators Architects.

Utssav's ideas and strategic approach has created breakthroughs for many entrepreneurs by saving them money, opening up new niches and creating opportunities for them. In architecture, he introduced Inventive Architecture framework that created a string of projects with unconventional design approach, that are now regarded as one of their kinds, are impactful and have changed status quo.

He has studied Architecture from Delhi and London with honors and has been an entrepreneur since. Coming from a family of architects, he was exposed to the profession at a very young age and saw various facets, contrasts and contradictions that influenced him in his quest. Over the years, Utssav has researched, studied and analyzed businesses, products and services from many verticals for their strategies, USPs and market dynamics in the context of innovation. This completely transformed his idea of what innovation can do and why businesses are stuck.

He is a strong advocate for disruption by design and believes in building out of the box solutions through a mindful analytical approach.